GREEN TECHNOLOGY

EARTH-FRIENDLY INNOVATIONS

Geeta Sobha

ROSEN
PUBLISHING®

Is Green Technology Necessary?

Each year, energy use in the United States increases, driving the need for more fossil fuel and increasing the harmful effects to the environment. As pollution and the rising cost of energy sources become worldwide issues, people are being urged to be more aware of how they consume energy. World leaders are pushing for cheaper energy-saving technologies. They also are calling for technology in the form of energy sources that will outlast the fossil fuels upon which most people are dependent. In addition to being cost-efficient, this technology, called green technology, must be environmentally friendly. That is, these new energy sources must not add to pollution.

Many organizations and scientists are working to call attention to the need for green technology. As people become more aware of the necessity of efficient energy sources, they are demanding alternatives to current sources. Renewable energy is one of the most important aspects of green technology. Solar power, biomass energy, and wind power are some of the "earth-friendly" alternatives that are being explored as ways to cut back on the use of fossil fuels. In addition, these energy sources will not add to pollution and its effects, especially global warming.

Current Sources of Energy

Electricity, fuel for vehicles, oil for heating homes, and gas for cooking and heating mainly come from coal, oil, uranium, or natural gas—all nonrenewable energy sources. These four nonrenewable sources are the greatest sources of energy in the world. Coal, oil, and natural gas are considered fossil fuels because they are the result of the decomposition of plants and animals that were alive millions of years ago. Uranium, a metal found in the earth, is used to produce nuclear power. Fossil fuels are constantly at work in our lives. We use them to produce light, heat, and power. They will eventually be used up, however. As they become scarcer, they will become more expensive. Today, we are already seeing oil prices increase.

Fossil fuel sources are not good for the earth's environment. In their production and during their use, environmentally harmful chemicals and gases, especially

The coal shown here, at the Niagara Mohawk steam station in Dunkirk, New York, is used to produce power.

carbon dioxide, are released. At times, important areas where animals live become polluted and even destroyed. Though nuclear power does not release harmful gases into the environment when it is burned, it is not considered to be a green energy source. It has the possibility of other dangers, such as the damaging effects of nuclear power plant meltdowns. These detrimental effects, as well as the fact that these fuels are not renewable, are driving the need for alternative energy.

Global Warming

The most notable harm to the environment caused by pollution is global warming. Global warming is an increase in the temperature of the earth's atmosphere due to too many polluting gases being trapped there. If the earth's atmosphere heats up too much, there will be many negative results. Warmer atmospheric temperatures will cause glaciers to melt and water levels to rise, leaving people on small islands and coastal areas

Global warming is affecting areas where polar bears live, causing ice to melt and reducing their hunting grounds.

homeless. Animals that depend on cold weather for survival in places such as the Arctic may disappear forever. In addition, as oceans warm up, animals living in those waters may die off. Warmer ocean temperatures will affect how some fish species breed. Ocean waters also influence the weather, and warmer waters will result in increasing storm frequency. In fact, global warming will cause an ongoing chain of reactions because the plants and animals that live on the earth are dependent on one another.

What Is Being Done

While most people agree that new energy sources are needed, there have been many debates about how to go about developing and bringing these sources into use. In some cases, cost may be the deciding factor in whether an alternative energy source should be used. Another factor may be that the technology is not readily available.

Concern over rising gas prices, as well as dependency upon foreign oil, have caused the U.S. government to consider alternative energy sources. The U.S. Congress is considering fuel-choice bills. These bills would offer car manufacturers special benefits such as tax breaks for building fuel-efficient vehicles. Right now, tax breaks already exist for people who use solar electric and wind power systems. People who use bicycles and electric cars also can receive tax breaks. Some states give money to people who are using alternative energy. The bills call for the United States to lessen its use of foreign oil.

On the opposite side of these financial incentives is the carbon tax. This tax is a fee on energy use, such as gas for a car or electricity in a home, that releases carbon dioxide into the air. The money usually is put into developing green energy sources and educating citizens about green energy. In April 2007, Boulder, Colorado, became the first U.S. state to start applying this tax. The city decided to reduce its carbon emissions based on the terms laid out in the Kyoto Protocol. The tax is an additional $1.33 a month for homes and $3.80 for businesses. People who use alternative energy sources receive a reduction on the tax, depending on how much they use. Other countries around the world, including New Zealand, Sweden, and Finland, already have begun to use the carbon tax as a way to reduce pollution.

The U.S. Energy Policy Act of 2005 created many guidelines for developing new energy sources that will increase vehicle fuel efficiency and reduce pollution. Some of these alternative energies are ethanol and hydrogen fuel. The act calls for controlling the effects of energy use and production on the environment. It also wants people to use alternative energy sources, not just the traditional ones that they are accustomed to using.

Steps are not just being taken in the United States. Global warming and pollution are worldwide concerns. In 1997, in Kyoto, Japan, 180 countries signed the Kyoto Protocol. The Kyoto Protocol is an agreement between these industrialized countries to cut emissions of gases that contribute to global warming and pollution of the earth's atmosphere. Every country has its own goal for the amount of emissions to be cut. Between the years 2008 and 2012, the target is to drop emission levels to 5.2 percent of what they were in 1990. That may not seem like a lot, but considering the number of factories and cars producing pollution worldwide, that target will not

be easy to reach. President George W. Bush refused to ratify, or endorse, the protocol. Instead, he put forth a plan that calls on U.S. businesses to cut emissions on a voluntary basis by 2010. His decision was not popular with many people around the world.

Green Energy Politics

The debates surrounding green technology center on whether there is really a need to develop alternative energy sources. Some people believe that human activities, especially the use of fossil fuels, are responsible for the warming trend in the earth's atmospheric temperature (global warming). Others believe this warming is a natural phase of the earth's cycle. Scientific evidence is heavily on the side of those who believe that global warming is happening. Measurements of gases in the atmosphere show that the levels of these gases are higher than they should be.

Another debate is whether the use of fossil fuels should be reduced. Some people think that there is a need to reduce fossil fuel use to conserve the fuels and reduce pollution. Others, meanwhile, are concerned about the financial effects on consumers and the

Industry is responsible for much of the carbon dioxide released into the atmosphere, contributing to pollution.

People dressed as polar bears protest against exploration of oil in the Arctic National Wildlife Refuge.

national economy. The people who are against conservation worry that conservation efforts will increase energy prices. Higher energy prices will affect many aspects of the population's daily life, including finances and income.

This financial issue leads to another discussion regarding oil. There are vast oil fields in areas of the United States. The government is hesitant to drill in these reserve areas due to possible negative effects on wildlife and the environment. On the other hand, these U.S. sources of oil could lessen the country's dependency on foreign oil, while increasing jobs. Yet another side argues that to open up these reserves is just a temporary solution, since this oil eventually will be depleted. Those who put forth this argument say that the answer is to develop and utilize alternative energy sources.

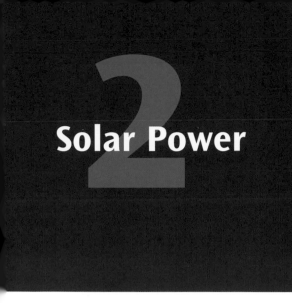

Solar Power

Solar power—power that is derived from the sun's energy—is becoming more and more popular as a renewable energy source. In harnessing solar power, no harmful gases are released, so there is no damage to the environment.

People have used the sun's energy for thousands of years. For example, the Anasazi people, who existed in North America from 1200 BCE to 1300 CE, built their cliff dwellings facing south so that they could capture heat from the sun during winter months. Hundreds of years later, in 1767, Horace de Saussure, a scientist in Switzerland, built a solar oven. In 1860, Auguste Mouchout, a French mathematician and inventor, began to work on applying solar energy to mechanical uses.

The first solar cells were invented in the 1950s by Russell Ohl at the Bell Labs. Before the 1970s, the majority of solar energy use was in space exploration programs. However, the oil embargo of 1973 pushed Americans to seek new energy sources. Solar power was one of the sources that people began to see as a means of moving away from oil.

The development of practical solar energy has been slow, as it has not been easy to capture sufficient energy to provide power efficiently. For a long time, fossil fuels generated much more power than solar energy. (Even today, coal is used to produce more than half of the electricity used the United States, while solar-produced electricity accounts for about 1 percent.) This is one of the reasons why, in the past, people were not enthusiastic about switching to solar power. However, solar technology has improved greatly. Solar power is becoming more efficient, cost effective, and accessible. People also are learning just how easily they can use the sun's energy. Some people who are building new homes include solar energy–producing cells in their designs. Others have designed their homes to be entirely powered by solar energy.

Photovoltaic Cells

Solar power is used to provide energy for many things. Some billboards, public telephones, and calculators are solar-powered. Or you may have solar-powered lights in your backyard that need no batteries or electrical wires. These items get their solar energy from photovoltaic cells. *Photo* means "light," and *voltaic* means "electric."

The roof of the house, above, uses solar panels to collect energy from the sun and supply it with power.

Photovoltaic cells, also called solar cells, use semiconductors to transform energy from the sun into electricity. Most semiconductors are made of silicon that can soak up the energy from the sun. Solar cells can be arranged into modules that will produce electricity in the form of direct current (DC). This then can be changed into alternating current (AC), which is the type used in homes. A device known as an inverter is used to convert direct current to alternating current. Electricity from photovoltaic cells can be shared or stored for later use.

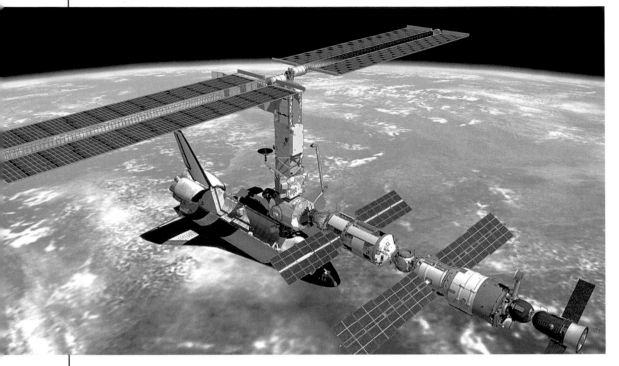

This NASA drawing shows the International Space Station in orbit. Its solar arrays capture the sun's energy and provide it with power.

Most solar cells are four-inch (ten centimeters) squares that can provide about two watts of electricity. Since this is a very small amount, solar cells often are set up in groups that will provide larger amounts of electricity. Small groups are referred to as solar panels and are used for homes, where they can be set up on rooftops. Solar panels also can be arranged together to provide even more electricity. Sizeable groups of solar cells, called solar arrays, are used for large outputs of power, such as for power stations supplying solar energy. The International Space Station uses solar arrays to generate power for its daily functions.

The average home needs about ten to twenty arrays to provide it with enough power. Once converted to electricity, solar power can be used in any part of a building that requires electricity. Hair dryers, refrigerators, DVD players, and computers can all be turned on effectively with solar-powered electricity. Power stations that produce electricity from the sun can be found in the United States, Germany, Italy, and Japan.

Collecting Solar Power

Solar power electricity generation is not much different from fossil fuel electricity generation. Power plants use fossil fuels to produce steam that turns turbines for creating electricity. Solar power stations use solar power to produce the steam to turn the turbines.

Solar power heating systems work differently than the traditional oil, gas, and electric systems. Buildings can be heated through two types of systems. One type collects heat in an air space that faces the sun during the day. It circulates and stores it for when it is needed. The second type of system collects heat through a wall with holes in it that also faces the sun.

The Pros and Cons of Solar Power

The major positive outcome of utilizing the sun's energy is reducing the drain on fossil fuels. Another plus is that solar energy can pay for itself in the long run. Once the equipment is installed, the energy that it produces is free. Though solar energy–producing equipment for a private home can be expensive, the amount of money saved by not paying monthly for oil-, coal-, or gasoline-produced energy can make up for the price of the equipment. The equipment also requires very little maintenance or repair once installed.

Some discouraging factors may include a complicated installation process and low power output on cloudy days. The direct current must be converted to alternating current, which most homes and businesses use. The arrays also need to be able to get full sunlight. If one photovoltaic cell does not get sun, it can stop current from all of the cells.

Who Is Using Solar Power?

Solar power is replacing traditional power in many places. Almost everyone uses some kind of charger these days, whether for a cell phone, an iPod, or another portable device. Solar-powered chargers can be used to recharge cell phones. The iSol is a solar-powered charger

Coney Island's Stillwell Avenue Terminal in Brooklyn, New York, is the largest aboveground subway station in the New York City subway system. The solar panels installed in its roof, part of a renovation completed in 2005, provide the station with about 250,000 kilowatt hours of energy in a year.

for the iPod. There are solar-powered holiday lights, security floodlights, and garden fountains. Small solar-energy devices can be used to power laptops. The beauty of all of these gadgets is that in order for them to work, all you have to do is expose them to sunlight.

Solar energy already affects our lives in many ways, even though we may not be aware of it. Space satellites use solar energy. Many bus stops in cities such as Seattle and Chicago are being lit by solar power. Solar panels often cover the tops of these bus stops. They collect solar energy during the day and work even on cloudy days. In Brooklyn, New York, one aboveground subway station gets all its power from a gigantic photovoltaic roof. As with the bus stops, the roof serves as both a shelter and a solar energy collector.

In 1997, a government program called the Million Solar Roofs Initiative was created to set up solar power systems in one million homes in the United States by 2010. By the end of 2002, the program had installed 350,000 solar power systems. State governments throughout the country have set up their own programs and installation goals that they will meet. North Carolina's Million Solar Roofs Partnership, for example, pledged to add 3,000 solar energy systems. In August 2006, California's governor, Arnold Schwarzenegger, signed a law that calls for one million solar roofs in his state by 2011.

Wind Power

3

Wind is created by the combination of the sun's heat hitting the atmosphere irregularly, the earth's rotation, and unevenness of the earth's surface. When air flowing over heated land rises, a vacuum is created. Cooler air moves in to fill the vacuum, and this moving air is what we call wind. In a way, wind is a form of solar energy, as it cannot exist without the sun's heat.

Wind turbines have been proven to be an efficient green technology. One wind turbine can generate enough electricity to light 30,000 100-watt lightbulbs. In 2004, California wind farms produced 4,258 million kilowatt-hours of electricity, more than 1 percent of the state's electricity. All over the country, wind turbines are being used to generate electricity, whether on a large-scale wind farm or by single turbines for private home use. The American Wind Energy Association reported that wind power generation grew by 27 percent in 2006 and is expected to increase by 26 percent in 2007.

Wind Energy

Windmills are one of the world's oldest renewable energy power sources. In 300 CE, they were used in Persia for pumping water and grinding grains. In the 1100s, the windmill was used in Europe for similar purposes. By the fourteenth century, Europeans also were using windmills to cut wood and make paint.

Windmill development continued throughout the centuries as changes in design were made to improve this energy source. When North America was settled, windmills were widely used. In the 1800s, many homes had small windmills for pumping water and for feeding farm animals. One windmill, the Aermotor, had such a successful design that it still exists.

Wind power is in use today, but with some changes. While early windmills performed physical duties, modern wind turbines are used to create electricity. The earliest electricity-producing windmill was made by Charles Brush of Cleveland, Ohio, in 1888. The first modern wind turbines were developed in the 1930s. These small turbines were used to charge batteries for homesteaders on the Great Plains. The large wind turbines that are currently used were developed through research in Europe and the United States. Each year, as the technology for wind turbines is refined, more and more wind energy is being utilized.

Wind Turbines

Wind turbines work like reverse electric fans: Instead of using electricity to make wind, wind turbines use wind to make electricity. These turbines are made of steel, and they all have the same basic design and parts: a rotor, nacelle, and tower.

The rotor is made up of two or three blades that turn when the wind blows. The larger the rotor, the greater the amount of electricity produced. The blades usually are made of fiberglass—a lightweight, sturdy material. The blades connect at the hub, inside of which there is a brake and a controller. The hub is connected to the nacelle. The nacelle is the main part of the turbine and holds a generator and a gearbox. The generator captures the turning blades' energy and produces electricity. The gearbox holds the parts that drive the generator. All of the parts are set on top of the tower, which is made of steel or concrete. Inside or next to the base of the wind turbine is a transformer that changes the electricity to the appropriate voltage for distribution and use.

Wind turbines range in size, depending on the needed output of electricity. Large turbines, producing megawatts of electricity, are used for wind farms. Small turbines for homes produce about 100 kilowatts. Small wind turbine towers can be 30 to 65 feet (9 to 20 meters) tall. Larger turbine towers can be 80 to 165 feet (25 to 50 m) tall.

Wind Farms

Wind farms are designated areas with a large number of wind turbines. The wind farms of Tehachi Pass in California, for example, have about 1,000 wind turbines each. The wind turbines work together with traditional electricity-producing technology, which is still needed for the times when there is not enough wind to move the turbine blades. The combination allows for a smooth, constant flow of electricity to homes and businesses. Wind farms provide power to an electrical grid, from which homes and businesses can obtain power.

The ideal place for a wind turbine is, of course, a spot that has a lot of wind. However, the flow of the wind must be steady without sudden gusts of stronger winds. The amount of wind necessary for moving wind turbines is about 10 miles (16 kilometers) per hour. The turbines stop operating when winds are about 55 miles (89 km) per hour because they can be damaged by extremely high winds. A braking system that is affected by high winds stops the turbines until the wind dies down. Then the brakes are released and the turbines begin to turn again.

These wind turbines are part of Great Britain's largest offshore wind farm. All together, the thirty turbines off the Great Yarmouth coastline in Norfolk, England, generate enough power for 41,000 homes.

The largest wind farm in the United States is the Stateline Wind Project in the northwestern part of the country. Other large wind farms in California include Altamont Pass and San Gorgonio. These wind farms are all situated in places where there is a great amount of wind. The Jersey-Atlantic Wind Farm in New Jersey is the first wind farm built along a coast in the United States.

Sweden, Denmark, the United Kingdom, Ireland, and Holland all have offshore wind farms that take advantage of high wind areas away from land. Offshore wind farms consist of wind turbines that are built into the seabed of areas that are less than 98 feet (30 m) deep. An offshore wind turbine is built just like a wind turbine on land, except that it is much bigger.

The Pro and Cons of Wind Energy

Wind power is one of the world's leading green technologies because it causes no harm to the environment. It does not produce greenhouse gases, and there are no toxic wastes. There are more than 70,000 wind turbines in the world, and the number keeps growing. Aside from the initial equipment costs, wind energy is free. In addition, unlike fossil fuels, wind will always be available. Access to electricity through wind turbines has improved the economy of rural areas by providing easy access to

Wind turbines stand over this farm near Alta, Iowa. Iowa ranks third in the nation with regard to wind energy; only Texas and California produce more.

energy. People such as farmers can have access to cheap electricity from wind power.

There are negatives to wind power production, however. The equipment can be expensive and may need repair when conditions such as power surges cause damage. Wind power needs to be applied in conjunction with fossil fuel power to work effectively, since wind speeds can slow down, therefore slowing down power production.

Some people consider wind turbines to be an eyesore, especially when situated in scenic areas. The turbines emit a hum that can be disturbing to people who live in the vicinity. These noises are being addressed by new turbine designs. In 2006, the Federal Aviation Administration (FAA) stopped fifteen wind farm projects in the Midwest after a study showed that they might get in the way of military radar.

Another major problem relates to wildlife living near wind turbines. Roads to wind farms can disturb animal habitats. Wind turbines are particularly fatal for birds and bats, as they are unable to see the moving blades of the turbines and often fly into them. Research shows that raptors are the most susceptible to flight-related injury and death. These environmental issues are being addressed by the careful choosing of wind farm sites.

The Cape Wind Project is a plan for an offshore wind farm in Nantucket Sound, near Cape Cod, Massachusetts. Supporters and opponents of this project are citing many of the preceding reasons for and against the building of this wind farm. If it is completed, the Cape Wind Project will be the first offshore wind farm in the United States.

Biomass and Geothermal Heat

Biomass energy currently accounts for almost half of the renewable energy sources used in the United States. Some sources predict that by 2020, biomass will account for 30 percent of the power used in this country. It is currently the fourth-largest energy source in the world.

What exactly is biomass energy? The term "biomass" refers to organic matter made from plants or animals. Biomass energy is produced through the burning of biomass and can be in the form of heat, electricity, or fuel. Biomass fuels can serve as replacements for gasoline, the fossil fuel that vehicles use for operation.

Plants, garbage, and wood wastes are most commonly used for biomass energy. However, many other forms of organic matter are used, including waste products such as tires, manure, seaweed, and straw. These things that usually are thought of as garbage can be turned into valuable energy sources. Gas created from decomposing garbage in landfills, called landfill gas, can be collected through pipelines to be used for the production of electricity. There will always be waste, and trees and plants can be grown, making biomass a renewable energy source.

How Biomass Energy Works

As a source of fuel, biomass energy is one of the oldest around. Just burning wood for a fire is considered a use of biomass energy. To create enough energy to provide electricity, however, wastes are burned at biomass power plants in large containers called hoppers. The heat produced from burning these wastes is used to boil water. In turn, the water's steam is used to turn turbines, which power generators to create electricity.

Paper mills are a good example of biomass energy in use. Instead of having to dispose of wood waste, the companies are turning the waste into electricity, running their operations and saving money. Several sugar mills are doing the same thing. Once sugar cane juice is extracted to make sugar, the pulp that remains is burned to create electricity to run the mills.

Anaerobic Digesters

Anaerobic digesters are used to treat wastes from sewage or to reduce the amount of garbage in landfills.

"Anaerobic" means to exist in the absence of oxygen. Within the digesters, bacteria are used to break down biodegradable garbage (material such as plastic cannot be broken down this way). This type of bacteria does not need oxygen to live and grow. Anaerobic digesters are used to produce biomass energy in the form of biogas. In this process, organic matter, like plants, is shredded and then processed in the digesters. Inside the digesters, the anaerobic bacteria break down the matter into methane, water, and carbon dioxide. This process takes place over a course of fifteen to thirty days. The biogas produced can be used to power the digesters themselves. The excess power can be sold to energy suppliers that sell this energy.

Ethanol and Biodiesel

Vehicles run on gasoline or diesel. These are forms of petroleum, a fossil fuel. In order to reduce the harmful gases released by burning gasoline or diesel, ethanol and biodiesel (both biomass fuels) are being combined with or replacing gasoline or diesel. Ethanol and biodiesel can be effective when it comes to cutting down the automobile emissions that are contributing to global warming.

Ethanol is an alcohol that is made from sugars in grain plants, including corn, rice, and wheat, and other

Certain varieties of corn are grown specifically for ethanol production. Above, signs mark different corn hybrids on a farm near Freeport, Illinois. A bushel of corn produces close to three gallons (more than ten liters) of ethanol.

plant matter such as sugar cane or cut grass. Gasoline that is as much as 24 percent ethanol can be used in today's cars. Higher amounts of ethanol require car engines to be altered. Most cars run on a combination of 8 percent ethanol and 90 percent gasoline, a blend known as E8. Brazil has one of the most successful ethanol programs in the world. There, citizens can buy cars that run only on ethanol. Most Brazilian gas stations have ethanol blends of E25 (25 percent ethanol and 75 percent gasoline) and 100 percent pure ethanol.

Biodiesel is an alcohol-based fuel that contains oils. These oils are not petroleum based. They can be vegetable oil, cooking grease, or animal fat. Through a chemical process called transesterification, glycerin is removed from the oils or fats, leaving behind a fatty acid known as alkyl esther, which is essentially biodiesel. Biodiesel can be combined with regular diesel or used in its pure form. Most biodiesel comes from plant sources such as soybeans. Some biodiesel makers recycle oils and grease from restaurants.

Geothermal Heat

Geothermal heat is generated from deep within the earth. The center of the earth is very hot, with temperatures of about 9,000 degrees Fahrenheit (4,982 degrees Celsius). This core heat dates back to the earth's very beginnings, more than four billion years ago. Proof of the earth's hot interior can be seen in the form of erupting volcanoes and geysers.

What exactly is geothermal energy? It is the use of geothermal heat as a source of energy. In ancient Rome, hot springs were used to heat homes. Thousands of years ago, Native Americans used geothermal heat

Cal Energy Generation operates ten energy-generating plants at its Salton Sea site in California's Imperial Valley. The plants, one of which is shown above, produce electricity solely from naturally occurring geothermal steam.

from hot springs' water to cook food and for medicinal purposes. Modern use of geothermal heat to produce electricity first occurred in Larerello, Italy, in the early 1900s.

In 1960, the first geothermal power plant opened in California and led the way for geothermal energy production in the United States. Today, most of the country's geothermal energy plants can be found in the West, especially in California, Nevada, and Utah. Hawaii also takes advantage of the geothermal power from the volcanic activity on its islands.

Around the world, other countries are using geothermal energy. Costa Rica, Kenya, the Philippines, Canada, and Japan are just a few of the countries that take advantage of this natural resource.

Taking Advantage of the Earth's Heat

Water from underground reservoirs lies below the earth in certain parts of the world. This water is heated by melted rock and magma from the earth's core, or center. Magma can be as hot as 2,200°F (1,204°C) and can heat water to about 700°F (371°C). Much of this hot water stays underground, as deep as 9,843 feet (3,000 m) below the surface. Some, however, reaches the surface of the earth in the form of hot springs or geysers.

Tapping into geothermal energy can be as simple as running the hot water through pipes and using it to heat homes. This technique has been used since the late 1800s. Heat pumps now are used for heating and cooling buildings. The pumps move liquid back and forth to pipes within the ground to cool or heat a building. This liquid can be water or water mixed with antifreeze. Antifreeze is a liquid that is added to water to lower its freezing point.

Temperature below the earth's surface is constant, at about 57°F (14°C). The liquid in the pipes gets warm from the earth's heat, and in the wintertime, heat is circulated to buildings. During the summer, the opposite happens.

The liquid picks up the warmth from the air in a building and sends it to the earth below.

Electricity from geothermal energy is one of the most successful green technologies. Hot water or steam from deep within the earth is used to create electricity. In one type of steam power plant, steam is sent through pipes to a turbine, which then uses a generator to make electricity. A flash steam power plant changes water at temperatures from 300° to 700°F (149° to 371°C) to steam, which is directed to a turbine and a generator to produce electricity. For areas where geothermal water temperatures fall between 250° and 360°F (121° to 182°C), the water is used to heat another liquid. The liquid, usually a chemical, then changes to vapor. The vapor affects the turbines in the same process as the other power plants that use steam. Then the chemical vapor is trapped, turned back into a liquid form, and used again.

Green Technology and Vehicles

Have you ever turned on the morning news and heard a reporter say to stay indoors due to a smog alert? Smog alerts often are due to air pollution in urban areas. Breathing in the unhealthy air can lead to health problems. Though cars are not the only producers of harmful gases, they contribute significantly. Consider the number of cars that are driven in just the United States each day. The San Francisco-Oakland Bridge, in California, for example, hosts as many as 250,000 cars daily. In and around Houston, Texas, about 2.5 million vehicles are driven every day. Cars that produce less pollution are especially important in cities. They can help reduce the frequency of smog alerts and breathing-related diseases and allergies.

The electric vehicle and the hybrid vehicle have become affordable and easy to operate, making them the most important green vehicles on the road today. In New York City, some city workers are using Global Electric

Motorcars (GEM) instead of gas-powered cars. These vehicles look a bit like golf carts and are perfect for driving short distances or in busy cities where there is a lot of slow-moving traffic. Some cities, like Berkeley, California, and Portland, Oregon, have charging stations for electric cars.

The hybrid vehicle uses both the traditional gas-powered engine and an electric motor to operate. It gets power from a battery within the car or from a fuel cell generator. Since the GEM relies on electricity (that most likely comes from a fossil fuel) and hybrid vehicles use petroleum-based gasoline, they both are relying on some form of fossil-fuel energy. However, they emit much less carbon dioxide than standard gasoline-powered cars.

Electric Vehicles

Inventors have been experimenting with electric vehicles for hundreds of years. In the 1830s, Robert Anderson of Aberdeen, Scotland, gave the world the first electric vehicle: an electric carriage. Around the same time, in the United States, Thomas Davenport built a practical electric locomotive. In 1891, William Morrison of Iowa built an electric wagon that could seat six people.

By the end of the 1800s, the London Electric Cab Company was using the Bersey Cab, a hybrid vehicle that used a battery and an electric motor. In New York City, the Electric Carriage and Wagon Company was using electric taxicabs. Most of the electric cars that were sold to private owners were luxury vehicles created for the rich. The electric car sold very well because at that time, cars with gas-powered engines were noisy, gave off fumes, and needed a hand crank to start.

The electric automobile was popular in Europe and the United States until a couple of inventions revolution-ized gas-powered cars. The self-starter did away with the need for a hand crank. In addition, Henry Ford implemented the assembly line for car manufacture in his factories. Ford's assembly line allowed him to make cars cheaply, and as a result, gas-powered cars became more affordable for buyers. Gas-powered vehicles took over the roadways by the 1920s and remained popular for the next sixty years.

In the 1960s, as the effects of pollution became apparent, the U.S. Congress first recommended using electric vehicles as a means of reducing car-related pollution. The 1970s' oil crisis further pushed Americans to find a way to reduce the consumption of fossil fuels. Many hybrid vehicles were introduced around this time. However, it wasn't until the 1990s that hybrid electric vehicles took off. Development of electric and hybrid automobile technology became more of an issue in the 1990s due to government policies such as the 1990 U.S. Clean Air Act and California's Zero Emission Vehicle

Above, a power cord hangs from the bumper of a Toyota Prius. The latest hybrids in development can be recharged at any household electric outlets and do not use any gasoline on short trips.

Mandate. Carmakers began to develop these two areas as demand for low-emission cars grew. In 1997, Toyota presented its hybrid vehicle, the Prius. Ford released the first American hybrid, the Escape Hybrid, in 2004.

Automobiles and Electric Technology

The technology of electric cars allows electricity to be stored in a battery pack, which is utilized by an electric motor. When the battery pack runs out of energy, it is plugged in and recharged. Any electrical outlet can be used to recharge an electric car's battery. However, recharging at a regular outlet requires about twelve hours. Charging stations, on the other hand, have equipment designed specifically for recharging electric car battery packs. Recharging at such a station takes about five hours. Heat from the brake system also recharges the battery. A controller manages the electricity from the battery to the motor.

A hybrid automobile uses a battery pack as well as a gasoline engine. These automobiles can turn off the gas engine and use the power created by the batteries. For example, hybrids can switch to the electric mode when stuck in heavy traffic or when waiting at a stoplight.

The design of hybrid vehicles also contributes to their energy-saving capabilities. Most hybrids are small cars, but larger sports utility vehicles (SUVs) are being sold today. Some, like Honda's Insight, use light materials for the body to reduce the weight of the vehicle. The tires are made to reduce air resistance when the car moves forward. Hybrids are designed to go as fast as necessary for everyday driving needs, including highway driving. These cars get the best gas mileage, however, on city streets where slower driving speeds are necessary. The electric mode is turned on when the cars are in stop-and-go traffic, and the gasoline mode takes over on highways.

So exactly who is using these vehicles? Look around your neighborhood. According to Reuters, in 2006, national sales of hybrid vehicles rose 28 percent. During this time, U.S. consumers purchased more than 250,000 hybrid vehicles. The Toyota Prius accounted for 43 percent of these sales, and remains the highest-selling hybrid in the United States. Other popular hybrids are the Toyota Camry and the Honda Civic. People buy new cars every day. Due to the rising cost of gas, along with its negative effects on the environment, some people are choosing to go with hybrids.

Delivery companies, such as Federal Express (FedEx) and United Parcel Service (UPS), are choosing hybrids. FedEx already is using hybrid delivery vehicles in New York City, Washington, D.C., and other cities around the country. In 2006, UPS tested a hydraulic hybrid, a new type of hybrid delivery vehicle. It depends on the frequent stops that a delivery vehicle makes. When the brakes are activated to stop the vehicle, energy is captured and stored. This is called regenerative braking. When the vehicle needs to move again, the stored energy is used.

Public transportation systems around the country have put much effort into buses that are more fuel-efficient and greener. New York City currently has the most hybrid buses in the United States.

In the September 2005 World Solar Challenge, this car from Southern Taiwan University was one of twenty solar cars that raced 1,860 miles (3,000 kilometers) across Australia's outback.

Solar-Powered Cars

Research on solar-powered cars is still ongoing, but a design that meets the needs of most car buyers has not been created. Solar-powered cars run on electricity that is stored in photovoltaic cells. Most of these vehicles have been created for research purposes or for racing. In fact, some people have made racing solar-powered cars a hobby. The World Solar Challenge and the North

American Solar Challenge are races that involve cars that use only solar power. Universities and car manufacturers are the participants in these races. General Motors' Sunraycer is a one-of-a-kind, solar-powered race car that has won many races. The U.S. Department of Energy is one of the sponsors of races like these, since the cars involve design and research that focus on an important source of green energy.

The Future of Green Technology

The green technology discussed so far seems to be our future when it comes to how we heat our homes, play video games, listen to MP3 players, and power every other aspect of our daily lives. There is no escaping the fact that fossil fuels will run out eventually. Meanwhile, according to scientists around the world, the polluting effects of burning fossil fuels are apparent already. Changes in weather patterns and melting ice in Arctic areas are just a couple of examples of the negative effects of the world's fossil fuel use.

Governments around the globe are looking to stop further environmental damage and find cheaper fuel alternatives to petroleum. President Bush, in his 2007 State of the Union address, asked Congress to support a policy called the Advanced Energy Initiative. This plan calls for the research and creation of new technologies and fuels. International agreements, such as the Kyoto Protocol, are further evidence that world leaders are taking a serious interest in the future of our global environment.

Fuel Cells

Many people believe that fuel cells are going to be as important to our future as fossil fuels are to us today. Fuel cells are the latest technological development that is being applied to make vehicles green. The first fuel cell was developed in 1843 by Sir William Robert Grove, a British judge and scientist. More than 100 years later, in 1959, Dr. Francis Thomas Bacon created a working fuel cell that produced five kilowatts of power, enough to operate a welding machine. The same year, Harry Karl Ihrig stacked 1,008 fuel cells together to give off enough power to operate a tractor.

In the early 1960s, the U.S. space program, the National Aeronautics and Space Administration (NASA), began to look for an efficient way of powering space vehicles. It decided that fuel cells were the way to go. NASA began using fuel cells for electricity on the Gemini and Apollo space capsules. All of NASA's space shuttle missions have used fuel cells to create electricity.

There are many types of fuel cells, but the most commonly used is the hydrogen fuel cell. This device is basically a battery. It puts out electricity as a chemical reaction between the hydrogen (the fuel) and oxygen that takes place within it. Water (which is drinkable!) is produced in the process. In fact, astronauts in the U.S. space program may drink this water while they are in

General Motors and the U.S. Postal Service have an extended agreement for testing the hydrogen fuel cell propulsion system in everyday driving conditions. In September 2006, the Postal Service began using the HydroGen3 fuel cell minivan in Irvine, California.

space. The fuel cell can be refilled with fuel when necessary. Hydrogen can be used in its gas or liquid form. As a gas, hydrogen is compressed under very high pressure and is kept in special containers. As a liquid, it is kept very cold: below –423.2°F (–252.8°C). The hydrogen fuel cell is the only fuel cell that does not give off any pollution. Other fuel cells, such as one that uses methanol, produce a small amount of pollution.

Fuel Cell and Automobiles

Fuel cell technology can provide power for many kinds of applications, from your cell phone to your laptop to your car. The fuel cell has become especially important in the automobile industry. Its technology has the greatest potential when it comes to reducing automobile pollution. Because the cell can be small and lightweight, its role in the future of zero- or low-emission vehicles is very significant. In the United States, the Freedom Car is a government project being developed along with many other fuel cell programs. The Energy Policy Act of 2005, for example, started a program to have hydrogen-powered vehicles available to the public by the year 2020. Other research continues worldwide.

Though cars that run on fuel cell energy are not presently for sale, in a few years this exciting technology could be available to all. Car companies currently are developing fuel cell vehicles. In 2006, Nissan announced that it will have a fuel cell automobile ready sometime after 2010. Honda says that it will have a fuel cell vehicle by 2008.

The California Fuel Cell Partnership promotes the use of fuel cell buses. In California cities such as Santa Clara and Oakland, buses that run on fuel cells are already in operation.

Green Energy and Money

Green technology will have a great impact on the financial world. Simple products, like solar-powered cell phone chargers, and higher technology, including cars that are able to run on pure ethanol, are all in our future. What and why we buy are affected by how we feel about our environment. Investors know this and are starting to pour money into green technology.

During the first three months of 2006, $357 million was invested in companies that create green energy. In November 2005, Bill Gates, one of the founders of Microsoft, invested $84 million into a company called Pacific Ethanol. There are also green investment companies. They only deal with the stocks of companies that are environmentally conscious for people who want to invest their money solely in those kinds of companies.

Large companies are changing the way they operate and the way they use energy. Companies such as UPS and FedEx are making important changes by buying hybrid vehicles. These two companies put numerous vehicles on the road every day, so using green vehicles will definitely save money as well as the environment. Xerox, a large company that makes a wide variety of office equipment and supplies, has cut down on energy use by creating a new way to produce toner.

Green Education

Since our future likely will be filled with green technology, new areas of the job market will continue to develop. Many students are exploring possible careers in green technology and are seeking to find the proper education and training for these careers. All of the alternative power industries will need workers in a variety of areas, from air quality engineers to auto mechanics specializing in green technology vehicles to construction workers who are able to build alternative energy homes. In the wind power industry, wind turbine specialists are needed to operate and manage the upkeep of the machinery. Electricians who specialize in installing solar-powered equipment will be in demand. Many workers also are needed in these fields to research and develop the technologies.

At various colleges and universities, classes in areas such as green energy sources and air quality are being developed for those who are interested in careers in the green technology industry. Some of the current educa-tion programs that can be applied to green technology include physics and electrical and chemical engineering. Some green technology companies even are offering

The installation of solar panels is a growing field, as many homeowners are seeking energy efficiency and turning to solar energy as a power source.

The Solar Decathlon, sponsored since 2002 by the Department of Energy's Office of Energy Efficiency and Renewable Energy, is a competition between twenty colleges and universities from around the world. Teams compete to design, build, and operate the most attractive, effective, and energy-efficient solar-powered house. Above, in October 2005, people tour a house built by Washington State University students.

scholarships to students who want to pursue a career in the field.

A Green Future

Access to cheap and simple power sources is something that modern society needs, and concerns about the management of energy use are on the rise. According to environmentalists, like former vice president Al Gore, who are putting significant effort into bringing the issue of global warming to the attention of the world, our current energy sources are damaging our planet. In the 2006 movie and accompanying book *An Inconvenient Truth*, Gore describes how the way we use energy is affecting a climate change.

By being aware of how our energy usage can affect our environment, we can take the right steps to apply green technology to our lives. Responsible energy use includes buying cars that run on an alternative fuel, as well as simply turning off a light or a computer when it is not in use. Turning on the television because a wind farm is providing energy or riding on a bus that does not pollute the atmosphere are just small steps on the way to a world that does not depend on fossil fuels. As the technology for renewable energy becomes more available and cheaper, green energy may very well affect every aspect of our daily lives.

Glossary

convert To cause a change.

current The movement of electricity through a wire.

diesel A thick oil that is used as fuel in diesel engines.

ethanol An alcohol that is used as fuel; also known as ethyl alcohol.

fiberglass A hard, lightweight plastic made of glass fibers.

fossil fuels Coal, oil, or natural gas formed from the remains of living organisms of prehistoric times.

generators Machines that change mechanical energy into electricity.

geysers Hot springs that send tall columns of boiling water up into the air.

global warming The process of gradual heating in the atmosphere caused by the burning of fossil fuels and industrial pollutants.

hydrogen A colorless, flammable gas.

magma Hot liquid matter below the earth's surface that can cool to form rocks.

mandate An official order.

megawatt One million watts.

methane A colorless, odorless flammable gas.

methanol An alcohol that is used as fuel; also known as methyl alcohol.

module Any in a series of standardized units for use together.

nacelle On a wind turbine, the nacelle holds the generator and gearbox.

photovoltaic cells Devices that produce electricity when exposed to sunlight.

pollution The presence of substances in the environment that are harmful.

raptors Birds that hunt other animals for food.

renewable energy Energy sources, such as wind or solar power, that cannot be used up.

semiconductors Substances through which heat and electricity flow more easily than through an insulator but less easily than through a conductor.

smog Fog and smoke or other pollutants in the air, such as exhaust fumes.

turbines Engines in which water, steam, wind, or gas pass through rotor blades to make them turn.

urban Having to do with a city.

For More Information

American Solar Energy Society
2400 Central Avenue, Suite A
Boulder, CO 80301
(303) 443-3130
Web site: http://www.ases.org

American Wind Energy Association
1101 14th Street NW, 12th Floor
Washington, DC 20005
(202) 383-2500
Web site: http://www.awea.org

The Canadian Centre for Energy Information
Suite 1600, 800-6 Avenue SW
Calgary, AB T2P 3G3
Canada
(877) 606-4636 or (403) 263-7722
Web site: http://www.centreforenergy.com

Canadian Wind Energy Association (CanWEA)
Suite 320, 220 Laurier Avenue West
Ottawa, ON K1P 5Z9
Canada

(800) 922-6932 or (613) 234-8716
Web site: http://www.canwea.ca

Sierra Club
85 Second Street, 2nd Floor
San Francisco, CA 94105
(415) 977-5500
Web site: http://www.sierraclub.org

Solar Energy Society of Canada, Inc. (SESCI)
McLaughlin Hall 406
Queen's University
Kingston, ON K7L 3N6
Canada
(613) 533-2657
Web site: http://www.sesci.ca

U.S. Department of Energy (DOE)
1000 Independence Avenue SW
Washington, DC 20585
(800) dial-DOE (342-5363)
Web site: http://www.energy.gov

U.S. Environmental Protection Agency (EPA)
Ariel Rios Building
1200 Pennsylvania Avenue NW

Washington, DC 20460

Web site: http://www.epa.gov

Web Sites

Due to the changing nature of Internet links, Rosen Publishing has developed an online list of Web sites related to the subject of this book. This site is updated regularly. Please use this link to access the list:

http://www.rosenlinks.com/itn/gtei

For Further Reading

Gunkel, Darrin, ed. *Alternative Energy Sources* (Current
  Controversies). Farmington Hills, MI: Greenhaven
  Press, 2006.

Hayhurst, Chris. *Hydrogen Power of the Future*. New York,
  NY: The Rosen Publishing Group, 2003.

Hirschmann, Kris. *Solar Energy* (Our Environment).
  Farmington Hills, MI: Kidhaven Press, 2005.

Naff, Clay Farris. *Wind* (Fueling the Future). Farmington
  Hills, MI: Greenhaven Press, 2006.

Parks, Peggy J. *Global Warming* (Our Environment).
  Farmington Hills, MI: KidHaven Press, 2004.

Passero, Barbara, ed. *Energy Alternatives* (Opposing
  Viewpoints). Farmington Hills, MI: Greenhaven
  Press, 2006.

Smith, Trevor. *Renewable Energy Resources:
  Understanding Global Issues*. North Mankato, MN:
  Smart Apple Media, 2004.

Snedden, Robert. *Energy Alternatives* (Essential Energy).
  2nd ed. Chicago, IL: Heinemann, 2006.

Walker, Niki. *Biomass: Fueling Change*. New York, NY:
  Crabtree Publishing Company, 2007.

Bibliography

Encyclopædia Britannica Online. "Solar Cell." 2006. Retrieved September 22, 2006 (http://search.eb.com/ eb/article-9106046).

hybridCARS.com. "History of Hybrid Vehicles." 2007. Retrieved March 23, 2007 (http://www.hybridcars.com/ history/history-of-hybrid-vehicles.html).

Kruger, Paul. *Alternative Energy Sources: The Quest for Sustainable Energy*. Hoboken, NJ: John Wiley & Sons, Inc., 2006.

Layton, Julia, and Karim Nice. "How Hybrid Cars Work." HowStuffWorks.com. Retrieved November 2006 (http:// www.auto.howstuffworks.com/hybrid-car.htm).

Marshall, Matt. "Green Technology Energy Investments Hit Record." SiliconBeat.com. May 24, 2006. Retrieved October 20, 2006 (http://www.siliconbeat.com/ entries/2006/05/24/green_technology_energy_ investments_hit_record.html).

Microsoft Encarta Online Encyclopedia. "Electric Car." Retrieved November 19, 2006 (http://encarta.msn.com/ encyclopedia_761580732/Electric_Car.html).

Microsoft Encarta Online Encyclopedia. "Wind Energy." 2006. Retrieved November 30, 2006 (http:// encarta.msn.com/encyclopedia_761595567/ Wind_Energy.html).

Miller, Kimberly M. *What If We Run Out of Fossil Fuels?* (What If?). Danbury, CT: Children's Press, 2002.

New Mexico Wildlife. "Impacts of Wind Energy Development on Wildlife." January 2004. Retrieved December 3, 2006 (http://www.wildlife.state.nm.us/conservation/habitat_handbook/WindEnergyGuidelines.htm).

Ramsey, Dan. *The Complete Idiot's Guide to Solar Power for Your Home.* New York, NY: Alpha Books, 2003.

Reuters. "Hybrid Sales Rise but Growth Slowing." February 26, 2007. Retrieved March 9, 2007 (http://news.yahoo.com/s/nm/20070227/bs_nm/autos_hybrids1_dc_1).

Smith, Trevor. *Renewable Energy Resources: Understanding Global Issues.* North Mankato, MN: Smart Apple Media, 2004.

U.S. Department of Energy: Energy Efficiency and Renewable Energy. "ABC's of Biofuels." Biomass Program. Retrieved October 2006 (http://www1.eere.energy.gov/biomass/abcs_biofuels.html).

Index

About the Author

Geeta Sobha is a writer of nonfiction books for young adults. She also works as an editor in New York City.

Photo Credits

Cover (top, left) © www.istockphoto.com/dirkr; cover (top, right), pp. 37, 40 © Justin Sullivan/Getty Images; cover (bottom), p. 47 © David McNew/Getty Images; p. 4 © www.istockphoto.com/Tom Tomczyk; p. 6 © David Parsons/National Renewable Energy Laboratory; p. 7 © Ty Milford/Aurora/Getty Images; p. 10 © age fotostock/SuperStock; p. 12 © Timothy A. Clary/AFP/Getty Images; p. 13 Alcatel-Lucent/Bell Labs; p. 15 © www.istockphoto.com/Alex Timaios; p. 16 NASA Marshall Space Flight Center; p. 19 © Kiss + Cathcart, Architects; p. 21 © Gabriel Bouys/AFP/Getty Images; p. 24 © Matt Cardy/Getty Images; p. 27 © AP Images; p. 29 © Warren Gretz/National Renewable Energy Laboratory; p. 32 © Scott Olson/Getty Images; p. 34 © Peter McBride/Aurora/Getty Images; p. 43 © David Hancock/AFP/Getty Images; p. 45 © Yoshikazu Tsuno/AFP/Getty Images; p. 50 © Melanie Conner/Getty Images; p. 52 © Mark Wilson/Getty Images.

Designer: Tom Forget; **Photo Researcher:** Amy Feinberg